VERONICA

LEON McAULEY

LAGAN PRESS
BELFAST
1994

Published by
Lagan Press
PO Box 110 BT12 4AB, Belfast

The publishers wish to acknowledge the financial assistance
of the Arts Council of Northern Ireland in the production of this book.

A catalogue record of this book is available from the British Library.

ISBN: 1 873687 05 2
Author: Leon McAuley
Title: Veronica
Format: Paperback (138 mm x 210 mm)
1994

Front Cover Painting: 'Girl with Fan' by Daniel O'Neill (1970)
(Courtesy of the estate of Daniel O'Neill and the Ulster Museum)
Cover Design by Chris Best
Set in 10.5/13.5 Bembo
Printed by Noel Murphy Printing, Belfast

for the woman in my life

CONTENTS

CORN CIRCLES
for Pauline

Who would have thought
it could have happened here—
in Broughshane, of a Sunday—
whatever it was that wrought
this ripened field of barley

to a state of such perfection?
Giotto—the artist, not the satellite—
did this sort of thing with one hand tied
behind his back.
We're not only human. We're

capable of anything we put our minds to:
the Saturnalia of *Ireland's Saturday Night*.
It's not that I don't wish or care
for scientific fact or explanation.
It's just that I'd prefer

to let my imagination
wander. To dream
is as important as to know:
to love where we've been,
but still to want to go.

LEGACY

This is my legacy:
a deed-box of mahogany,

lined with green baize.
In it, a bunch of hopeless keys,

and, monogrammed with Ps,
four handkerchiefs,

one blue; for pure mischief
a linen anti-macassar

white as the driven snows.
All so familiar:

all stained
with a stain that hardly shows.

LAYDE

The invisible is angrier
than any tribe of Indians
who think their spirits
might be stolen.
Jealous of the camera

it feathers and foxes
along the skyline
and turns the sky to sepia,
fuchsia, grass a darker brown.
It is trying to gather

Otto Leyde's landscape
back to itself again.

And somewhere, near a place
called Crau or Grail,
we'll stop above the sea.
And slipping out of gear
will nudge us

like a half-forgotten sin.
I'll say, 'I don't know why—
those houses on the mountain
don't seem right.'
And you'll remember

Leyde's church and island
melting into light.

UPPER BUCKNA

A grey crow crucified on a barbed wire fence,
its limp head hanging.
It is, indeed, a warning
and makes a cruel kind of sense.

A grey fog clinging to a barren mountain top.
Upper Buckna, its walls precise and grim,
in the wilds of County Antrim:
each stone a full stop.

CRANFIELD

It must have been that hawthorn
put it in my mind,
its branches wrapped in tattered polythene.
It rattled and lurched in the wind,
wraith-like, torn, anguished, thin—
Cranfield, *Creamh-choill*,
'wild garlic wood', 'wood of wild garlic',
however English the name may sound.

Its tiny roofless church is heaven-roofed:
by day, with cloud; at dusk, with stars.
Its genteel floor—a green, distinguished, sward—
dried by the sun at noon,
is showered with a gentle rain
the whole year round.

Now jettied, Cranfield,
swanned and heroned,
swallowed and amazoned, Cranfield,
hushed. No wild, white garlic flowers.
A Holy Well, a leafless thorn-
bush, never out of leaf,
flapping with children's prayers,
mothers' and fathers' grief.

THE FAMILY GATHERED

No, I am
finding it increasingly difficult
to picture myself,
particularly to myself,
as the young rebel
I somehow
know I am.

I have children
myself now
and lay down the law—
as if by some sudden miracle
I know the law
myself, now
I have children.

Still and all,
I'd be lying
in the face of reality
not to admit the possibility
that sooner rather than later
I'll be lying
still, and all

the family gathered
round me—
the older generation,
the increasingly younger rebels—
as you lie here tonight,
still, and round us all
the family gathered.

BALLYMENA MON AMOUR

Stuck behind the bread van
behind the laundry van
behind the bin lorry

on bin day
in Cullybackey,
while other people's lives scurry

to school and office,
to do the shopping
in ghostly Ballymena,

the thin man's
precision
wrist-watch stopping

at 8.55 am
or 9.05
precisely.

The exact time
is irrelevant.
The negative capability

of a child's shadow
stalks the playground wall
among autumnal ash and lime

in Hiroshima,
on Main Street,
Nagasaki.

GOING BACK

Once more I pace myself
and take it from the top.
I read between the lines
and lines of tousled locks,
these tatty heads and those
full of conditioning:
my small anthologies,
a second generation.

Is this one *Shane*,
John, there, from *Moonfleet*?
I'm marking time again
in long iambics
that echo in my head
and rattle from my feet.
Above it all
I hear the slow clock tick.

Time's come to chide again.
I pick a theme:
berate them now
for writing on the desks,
retrace my footsteps
down the dusty floor
and shout and shout
until they've sanded blank
their wooden palimpsests.
I stare, give back
their blank expressions.
They never apologise—
a pride of fathers
staring from their eyes.

CALL

The man you think you know
is not the man you marry. Childless,
Call was alone at the family rosary.

He had the last of the tall ships,
sheet and topsail, fo'c'sle, shroud,
the best and tallest stories:

a drink in every bar-room,
a girl in every port, the best
of both worlds and the start of steam.

She had Patience, the wireless,
'Reports from coastal stations
at ten hours, Greenwich Mean Time:

Anglesey, wind veering westerly,
gusting to gale force at times'.
The best of good company. Her own.

In the Third Order of Saint Francis
the beginning and end of each day
was the laying out and contemplation

of the shroud, reminding one of death.
She was as good as married to Christ,
alone with him to bear her load.

He had sailed the deadly seas
from lust to avarice and back.
She supposed the money went on drink

or sport. Not that she wanted.
All summer long, blackcurrants filled
her garden at the shore; the hedges

running wild with brambles,
sea-salt drying in the air.
We picked rosehips together

with the sea-wind in our hair.
I sat in her lap all winter
learning my ABCs.

'Prestwick, west one, mist three miles,
1027, rising slowly, fair.
Ronaldsway, Killough, Kilkeel ... '

He came home a foreigner, polite, dour.
What was there to say?
Cupping the dog-end of a Woodbine

to his chest on his way
to the shop for a paper,
a tall tramp steamer trading

between the bookies and the bars,
sailing close to the wind.
He would not wear a collar.

Tonight, colder than lovers,
they are almost together.
Wind blows through the covering

of scutch grass and clover
beyond their silent bed. Solemnly
the wireless issues warnings

'of gales in the following places:
Sea Areas Dover, Ross and Cromarty,
Sole and Lundy, Fastnet, Irish Sea'.

BLATHACH

Patrick the traveller, footsore and weary,
arrived in Glenravel, parched with the thirst.
He asked them for buttermilk.
They refused his request.
Indignant, Patrick suddenly cursed.
He christened their mountain *Blathach*
that they might always be blessed
with buttermilk in their hungry valley.
Or so the story goes.

'Blathach,'
he says, 'you're there
and, by God, you will be there
if ever I come back.'

I follow the dry stone wall, the succulent red track
the sheltering sheep have squelched, to the running sore
of the mines half-way up Blathach,
where the men of Glenravel dug out iron ore,
and stand with my father and look back
across the valley to Skerry Rock,
up the stony loanin from the road to Crooknahay
Tuftarney, Knockanully, the small farms
where my father's people had their day.

'Blathach,'
my father says, 'you're there
and, by God, you will be there
whenever I come back.'

And things that I have heard, but never understood—
inheritance and ownership and law and faction fights,
bad blood between neighbours, run clear through him

like the water in this burn that springs from where we stand—
the purest and sweetest water in the whole of Ireland,
he claims. He'd tickled trout further down.
He blathers on of this and that and where and who
and what his father did and built and how he met his Waterloo
and why he was christened Patrick, and, always, in the end

'Blathach,'
he says, 'you're there
and, by God, you will be there
if ever I come back.'

WHAT I REMEMBER OF MY UNCLE BARNEY

What I remember of my Uncle Barney
is the soft hat and the whiteness of his head
like a goose egg when he took it off. The hat.
He hung it on his knee, as if he and it
had struck some sort of bargain. The hat.
He spat in his palm, shifted on the lumpy cushion
and laid into his fry.

He farmed the rushy mountains of Tuftarney,
which made me think of toffee,
and he called gooseberries *goosegogs*—
and the fact that it balanced and never fell.
The hat.

Not that he talked about *goosegogs*—
he talked about yows and withers
and the great weather it was for the sheep-sale
and how you always got great weather
for the sale in Cushendall.

And that he was curious. But
what I remember most of my Uncle Barney
is how the yolk of the fried egg
hung like an hour-glass,
between his nicotine-stained teeth,
and that it balanced and never fell—
as if he and it had struck some sort of bargain.

THE VERY SAME

As sure as sure,
when I was bought a crombie overcoat
they bought a crombie overcoat
for the eldest boy next door.

Nothing was ever said. When Christmas came
and I got a silver space suit,
he would get a space suit.
Year in, year out, it was always the same.

I would arrive at Mass one Sunday
tricked out in a coat with a velvet collar.
He would be tricked out in a different colour
of velvet, but the very same coat, the very next Sunday.

Then my mother had a brainwave. Hide and seek.
She rigged me up a cloak of invisibility,
much like Frigg's cloak of invisibility.
Last Tuesday. It worked like a dream.

Nobody's seen their eldest for a week.

THE SUICIDE PACT

I was nine when I made the suicide pact with my brother.
Perhaps it was remiss of me not to have informed him,
but at the time he was five years old
and not much given to introspection,
or, as my mother called it, 'thinking long',
being rather more inclined—though here
I may be doing him a wrong—to colonise my space-suit.

Since I had made up my mind that if either or both
            my parents died,
by arson, accident or civil war or nuclear holocaust, or act of God
(though burglary, gruesome torture, skulduggery
            and subsequent murder
I considered the more likely causes of loss of life, nuclear holocaust
in those days of Hiroshima, Lourdes and Fatima, coming
            a close second)
he would, unfortunately, be required to go and get the knife.

My problem was, of course, the knife. Ours were the spatula-
bladed, bakelite, cream-handled kind, useless
for anything more violent than spreading butter. Unless ...
I thought I might hone one down to a serviceable edge
by dint of a couple of Saturdays' loud, but diligent
scratching and scraping on the acute concrete angle
of our scullery window ledge.

One way or another, he was implicated.
I thought of the sharpened blade,
and how the glinting, criss-cross hatching
reminded me of the sky behind the mushroom cloud
in the films of the nuclear tests. And, though he was implicated,
my little brother slept peacefully beside me. I liked him sleeping,
unaware of what was before him. He had the look of an angel.

THE GOOSE WING

Miss Duffy is an angel.
With a chalk-white whisk
she is fluffy-dusting her books, her angled desk,
the porcelain outer ring of her ink-well
with its iridescent crust of oak-gall ink.

I think of a bull's-eye and I think of Saturn,
I remember the blue knuckle and the blood-red ulcer
on the bone-end of her goose wing.
She sips scalding black tea from a thermos flask,
scolding to herself. She finishes in a jiffy.

Once more her wing-tip
sweeps across Ulster
scratching the dust off grey
Belfast and green Tyrone, Lough Neagh—
itself torn from the oxter of an angel.

JACOB

The angels walk
all over me
as softly and as free
as the light
falls through my window
or the wind
blows through the trees.

Nor am I more diminished
by these gentle victories
than the singing of the wind-harp
when the wind falls to a breeze
or the wild ducks disappearing
to their northern territories.

But this wrestling with pure spirits
is a solitary kind of sin:
you're forever wrestling angels
and the angels always win.

BUNDORAN

That's me at the back with my yacht
and the itchy, yellow bathing-suit
covered with white yachts.

And that girl's my cousin, Bernadette
(I called her *Bundo*) on the beach at Bundoran
(couldn't quite get my tongue round Bernadette).

Bundo. And that old lady
in the sun-dress with the polka dots
is Aunt Susie. Scarlet and white spots—yes

I remember it like yesterday—that sun-dress.
Blind most of her life, Aunt Susie.
Cataracts.

There are dozens of us here.
Me in various stages of embarrassing undress
on every beach where I tipped up a sandcastle

from here to Pan's Rocks: each waterfall
where water ran and I ran and Bundo ran.
Bundo. Bernadette.

And mothers and aunts in sunglasses and sun-frocks.
Always smiling. Aunt Susie. Blind, and always smiling,
and the sun always shining, over her shoulder, black.

GARLIC

Is sacerdotal, clothed in stiffened silk
and not without its sting. Is said
to purify the blood. Is parcelled
in a brittle quick you can't draw back.

In the kitchen I sang
as I split the clove,
and the kettle was singing
on the stove

for garlic is whiteness
tinged with mauve,
dry as bone; clutched tight
to emptiness, a baby fist

touched, like a relic,
to throat and wrist
and bloodstained and fanged
and very much in love.

THE ATOMISER

One thing led to another,
and when—you spendthrift you—when,
with extravagant spit and spume,
you atomised the back of my hand
and along my wrist-bone
with your spindrift and the mizzling rain
of your immaculate perfume,
then touched it to your own,
you made us blood brothers.

THE NEW HOUSE

Dawn. The New House yawns
and stretches out
its wash-day arms
in a sisterly way.

Spring breezes out and in.
Above is the South.
The hazel in the Rassan
speak in tongues.

Mayfly accumulate
and take a turn
across the water
next the stream.

The smoke says Murray
will be burning whin.

Over the border little clouds
of Rice's lambs
stray down the waves
of grass on the Castle Hill.

Wet trickles darken
down the Street:
the priest at Faughart
rings for Mass.

The bell of darkness ebbs
and flows about your feet.

Clover and primrose
dapple your morning talk,
foxgloves. Life is good.
Yours is an open book.

THE PRESENT

At this particular cusp or node
in the space-time continuum,
with Poland looming large,
Afghanistan, Gaddaffi,
Reagan, Bush, Saddam,

the whole wide world,
the Gulf, the Ayatollahs,
all playing hell with my love-life
and the arms talks
stalled, as usual, in Geneva

(not that you *give* a damn,
your light is off
and you've lost track of time)
you arch your back.
'I'm going to explode!'

you scream. 'Hush now ...
think of the neighbours.' 'Neighbours?
My Mushroom Cloud! My Atom Bomb!'
'*Mush*room cloud? *Atom* bomb?
O come now, come now, come ... '

THE HARMONIUM

I am sitting at our second-hand harmonium
with my daughter on my knee,
(for fathers have their uses)
pedalling frantically, while she

free-wheels down intricate variations and abuses
of, she claims, *Twinkle Little Star.*
And as the second hand becomes the hour
and she still tickles

the nicotine-stained ivories
and I still turn the swallows in the eaves
I try to persuade her that a)
the only tune

this damned harmonium knows
is *Bringing in the Sheaves*,
and that b) it's my turn.
'Less is more,' I chorus.

'Lovely, my lovely Alice, leave it there.'
I want a burst of Haydn, say, *The Clock.*
But no. She will have her fling.
Less *schön* than Schönberg, more

Bela Lugosi than Bartok.
All art, as Pater says
(though not as in *pater familias*)
aspires to the condition of music,

but, being domestic
and imitating life, *meine Liebling*,
our art, Alice, aspires
to the condition of cycling.

[35]

GHOSTS

A child who was a shadow bursts
from the curtains' figured lace.
The room goes dark again.

They pick the middle of the day
for being ghosts. Your voice
has become a high-pitched shriek

of concern for linings,
pelmets, *Swish*. The children
swirl our curtains into cloaks.

The big one tells about the day
she saw the stranger on the landing.
She uses words you know she doesn't know—

his hair was a helmet, his face was smoke—
she will stand the way she saw him standing.
You cannot bring yourself to look.

SÍ BEAG, SÍ MÓR
for Maggie

'Once upon a time there were two mountains.
A big mountain and a little mountain.
Make the two mountains.
In a world that was almost as flat
as the first day of Creation.
Make the mountains.'

Beneath their quilt,
my two sons bend their knees
and there are, suddenly,
two mountains.
A big mountain and a little mountain.

'And from the top of the big mountain,
you can see across the whole of the six counties
from the bushes of Tyrone to the glens of Antrim.

And on the little mountain there lived
a shepherdess, with a hundred thousand sheep.
And she was slender, tall and sprightly
as the sally rod she used to drive her sheep
lightly hopping and jumping and wriggling,
their tails bouncing and wagging,
down the valley between the two mountains.
Here they come now, here they come—let's count them.'

And the three of us count them
until unrest stops in the drumlins of Armagh
and their breathing
steadies to the dim sound of the waves
beneath the Temple of the Winds at Mussenden
and far away Benone.

And I can sneak away, and into bed myself,
where,
once upon a time,
there were two mountains.
And a shepherd lived on one of them
who had a million, million sheep,
and he was thick and lumpy
as the knotted blackthorn stick
with which he used to drive them.
And here they come now, lightly
hopping and jumping and wriggling,
their million, million tails
bouncing and wagging.
Count them. Count them.

THE SWAN

What if I plunged, elbow-deep, my hand,
let's say, my alabaster hand,
behind your neck, way, way deep down
into that thicket of weighty emptiness
you clamp between your icy wings?

What would I find?

Sticking plaster, hanks of itchy string,
dozed elastic bands, a mildewed half-a-crown,
a clutch of library tickets from 1986,
a stamp torn off for some forgotten charity.
Ordinary, useless things? Let's see. Go on.

Are you sure you wouldn't mind?

FIONNUALA'S DREAM

From the deep down of her sleep
Fionnuala stretches a graceful arm above her head
so high her fingers almost touch the ceiling.
She has been dreaming, dreaming
a gentle dream. She was a swan.
Her head was proud and steady,

her neck was white and long.
She drifted, bobbing up and down
and down and up on the magic lake
of the looking glass above the deep-
blue mountain of her headboard.
The current ran cold and teasing

across her belly and her legs, like someone
tugging gently at her less-than-pristine sheet.
She shivers. She stirs slightly,
half-dreaming, half-awake.
Across the room, the breathing of her brothers
ebbs and flows like wavelets.

They could sleep for hours yet.
Aedh, Fiacra, Conn: their dreams
are dreams of hurler, spear-chucker, charioteer.
Aedh snores. A snort.
She loves her sleeping brothers in their sleep.
Three heads above that wave that, always breaking,

never breaks. Three small heads:
one silver, one darkening, one gold.
Soon she will rub the sleep out of her eyes,
get cold, get up, and tip-toe to their bed.
Six shoulder-blades, so delicately formed
they could be sprouting wings.

Three angels. What's this you call them?
Thrones, Denominations, Cherubim and Seraphim.
Where did these words come from?
She does not know these words. They drift
in her mind as leaves drift on a river—ash leaves
that float beneath an oak-tree from somewhere far upstream.

Angels. But now they kick and toss and wake
and, human again, they boast and punch,
all arms and chin, shoving
and thumping each other with pillows until the room
is a blizzard of feathers, a snow-blowing,
and mother will have to come in.

THE CHILDREN OF LIR

I claim as my own special property
the legend of *The Children of Lir.*
I guard it with some jealousy.
I stake my claim by vir-
tue of the incontrovertible fact
that I was brought up in Cushendall
on the shore of the North Channel
which was, in the mists of antiquity
(which differ from contemporary mists
in almost every quality,
and in none more so than their mystery)
of course, the Sea of Moyle.

I can, therefore, speak with some authority
on every aspect of the swan.
I have sought out and made careful study
of the swan everywhere I could find one.
I have sat by the Six Mile Water
and the shores of Lough Neagh
and watched them walk on water, swim the air,
noting the set and disposition of each muscle
(not that these swans in their off-white reality
bear any but the slightest similarity
to those great white swans of legend).

Fionnuala, with her brothers, I aver it, she
would have spurned the titbits we
throw at these shadows from our crisp-bags
as we stand laughing with our children,
amazed at their burgeoning humanity,
savouring their accuracy, their dexterity.
Largely we ignore the swans. Posterity
will not easily forgive us. It stands accusingly

even now and stares with its empty crisp-bag.
I have become expert, too, concerning chains.

Though my wife originates from Silverbridge
and therefore her native myth
and orthodoxy, for what it's worth
is the comings and goings
and to-ings and fro-ings
of the Gap of the North,
she is a Lirite too, taking to the faith,
as I often say, like a swan to water.
We have two sons and a daughter

and while we now live in Ballymena,
they have been brought up strict Lirites.
Indeed Fionnuala—that's my daughter's name—
sits up late into the night with me, discussing chains.
We find, in chains, an uncanny relevance
to contemporary life. We are convinced
that this is not simply coincidence or mere chance.
Distance, for example, is measured out in 'chains':
people speak of 'chains' of atoms—'chains' of events.

But we have our enemies. We are an enclave
of Lirites trapped between the mad Sweeneys,
the Sons of Uisneach and the followers of Medbh.
They purport to despise us and lose no opportunity
to cast aspersions, if nothing worse.
'How can you be a Lirite, you, born in Dungannon?'
which I must admit is true—'For heaven's sake
your father's from Glenravel!'
True again. But I have my answer:
for I am a Child of Lir—
and we were born to travel.

THE IBIS

I

Is it really three thousand years
since they buried the little Pharaoh
whom we deified?
Battened the hatches once and for all
on sweet king Tut
and threw the key away?

In that last ray of sun
that glanced from his golden brow
our priests have lined
the sweating eunuchs up.
The soldiers lance them down
into a moistening pit.

The start of another day
is staining the desert red.
You are transfixed:
your heavy breathing
mists the icy desert air.
I am crystal.
I stand quite still.

Sigh me a silver ghost
or crimson in the shadow
of your side.
But for the roll
and twinkle of your eyes
I could believe you
mummified.

II

It moves like someone's hand
beneath your jumper now:
history of shifting sands,
of mountains, sea and ice,
landlocked as a monster
in a lukewarm foreign loch.

A kind of disbelieving
is the furrow that it ploughs.
It starts at dawn
from reeds or meadows
like a lark,
a tight, rosy curlew

that grows into a stork
and circles near
the cold chimney
of our house.
It gathers itself
to see if it might settle here

and start another life.

GAE BOLG

This is a new little God,
wiry, working for himself
in a smallish way:
livid with the power
in a cough, the eyelid's
smallest flicker, to make
his people laugh or cower
in the sweating darkness
of a corner. His drinking
goes right to their heads.

Here are the little tricks
he has perfected:
putting the lesser planets
on the long finger, spinning
them round and round the black;
blessing the white moon
in its crescent, dusting
the lighter blue
of his young heaven
upon the milky earth.

By now he will know the how
of the Hero's Salmon Leap,
the why and the wherefore
of endlessly kissing the pink.

So, taking his cue from way, way back,
as far as Finn or as Cuchulain,
he makes his world to hold its breath,
a balloon full of water, swollen,
fit to burst. The long-drawn start
of his spasm, the head-on crash

of skull on skull, scatters the stars,
sends frightened fauna running
to the far-flung corners of his empire,
the flat green plain, his emptying domain.

THE IRISH WEREWOLF

Just happens
to be a vegetarian
with an idiosyncratic,
though predictable, constitution.

The only visible sign
of his inherited condition
is that with the new moon
his hair begins to whiten.

He suffers from constipation—
he cannot pass a lay-by.
He answers every question
with an enigmatic, 'Maybe ... '

A PAIR OF HANDCUFFS

You know what it's like
when you don't want to, or haven't the time
and you say you're all tied up. That may work fine
for people like you and me. Cuts no ice with Houdini.
Without handcuffs and gag, straitjacket and chain, he
would have been lost for work, if not for words, and we
would have lost an emblem for our age.
Both artist and escapist, he turned
our claustrophobic nightmare into mime.
Dark circles round cherubic eyes,
Harry Houdini, sage enough to see
how handcuffs, by their very nature, rhyme.

KNOCK, KNOCK

Through the electronic wizardry
of a static-ridden PA
the clergy trumpet Armageddon—
this might be Judgement Day.

Weapons of mass destruction mass
on the borders of every state
and among the tawdry relic stalls,
'How's business?' 'Going great!'

My mother-in-law collects souvenirs
of the Mother-of-all-Battles
to give to her friends in Crossmaglen
to place with their goods and chattels.

Rejecting the giant rosary beads
and Bouquet of Masses forms,
I choose instead, a Made-in-Taiwan
Madonna-of-All-Snowstorms,

who, trapped in her plastic bubble,
with scarcely room to sneeze,
conjures internal blizzards, like me,
with seemingly consummate ease.

THE WHITE LADY

Less the sea-stack,
more the perfect lady.
Peer across her puffed shoulder
to her sisters and brothers,
the rocking clouds that boulder
Sphinx-like over Mull.

Mother of our last days,
keeping her cool;
hampered as Fionnuala,
being a swan,
waiting for the pull
of wing, at last, to slacken.

Then she'll step across the road
in a rustle of watered silk,
a fleeting ermine trim, to cool
a newly lissom wrist
in the Sea of Moyle,
her wrinkling crinoline.

THE ICON

'He's a Russian.
What can you expect but blasphemy
from a Russian?' And there is the icon

on the television set:
a black square on which a scarlet square
is having itself a pirouette.

She has no time for anything
as trivial as art. 'Forget this foreign nonsense.
Put your faith in the Sacred Heart.'

She is interested in Faith.
I am interested in the tradition
that says a picture placed

across the corner of a room becomes an icon:
how things can have meanings other than they seem
in a certain place at a certain orientation.

I am suddenly aware
of the void behind our television.
The dusty, dim, triangular fall

suggestive of The Trinity,
of the name of a woman I can't put a face to,
of infancy, incontinence, infinity.

THOUGHT BUBBLES

A lady in a snowstorm,
a goldfish in a bowl,
a spaceman in his helmet,
a diver in a shoal

of goldfish.
A baby in an incubator,
a pilot in a Spitfire,
your scent in an atomiser,

a saint at a country shrine
wrapped in polythene,
the man I loved in his oxygen tent,
now distant and serene.

SPEEDWELL

The moon, as she hunkers here, in the plush of this garlic dell,
all but astounds her, and this morning's quiet magic,
the dark, the damp green smell. Still not quite able to forget
her hunger for normality—Japonica and cordonned pear

and the overweening logic of the gravelled *parterre*
of privet and clipped laurel. How very much she cares to be
cocooned and cherished. Surrounded by careful spontaneity:
tight-lipped burdens of veronica, insinuations of speedwell.

BRAILLE

Their staring always
cuts you down to size.
When it comes to kissing-
time, and the girl
closes her eyes,
it's the Real McCoy
and trouble probably.

You try to keep an open mind
when she says, 'Love, if it is real,
is always pure and kind.'

You stand there, stock-still,
open-mouthed, sock-eyed,
trying—or trying not—to graze
the soft braille of breast,
the closed book of thighs.

THE VEIL

Had she done all she could?

Somewhere she found the strength
to lift her apron
and engage his head:
the moving weight of stone,
the heat of new-baked bread.

What had he left her?

All a man can leave a girl:
his broken sigh, his wounded love,
an apron soaked
in sweat and blood,
the spit and image of a God.

VERONICA

I

The Background

To be blunt
it's the colour of cow dung:

neither wall nor vista,
neither stucco, sea nor sky.
Behind the wine crushed-velvet curtain,

the indeterminate perspective
of her recent history
measures itself, uncertain

in distemper.
An unearthly mixture
of earth and air.

It's common knowledge,
neither near nor far.
Her past retains its homespun mystery:

the thundery clouds
of her personal *Götterdämmerung*
are neither here nor there.

II

The Vase

Among these tight-lipped burdens
of veronica, one wonders ...

the odd stray leaf of elder flower
(*boortree*, we would say) wanders,

straining for her shoulder.
I follow the line, a thirsty eye
that yearns to turn to wine
the unassuming water of her dress.

Hyacinth simpers, violet fuchsia
blushes, iceberg roses sigh.
Such vortices of inward-looking love!
Thought bubbles, syntheses of passion,

convoluted energies of ice!

III

The Head

She takes on the air of an icon. Her hair
a river of night on which the moon
reflects: serene, compassionate, bright.

She's all made up!
The charcoal smudges of her eyes
are charcoal smudges, nothing more:

that shy come-hither look of hers
is wishful thinking—
and the wishful thinking's yours.

IV

The Eyes

Bracket,
quote, unquote,
close bracket.

V

The Diadem

Her fierce corolla, her torc,
her fiery crescent moon—
... *a surface that rhymes*
with but is not
the Celtic thing.
The Claddagh ring.
A tammy, a duncher
to airie thinnesse beat.
She has been canonised
by far-fetched *dinnseanchas*—
the yellow pages

of the reprobate
Geraldus Cambrensis'
History and Topography
of Ireland. It sets her apart
from humanity,
creates a martyr
as Oswald's flattened bullet
created John F. Kennedy,
his airbrushed head on a plate,
above more Irish hearths
than the head of John the Baptist.

VI

The Bodice

Cradled in her awkward arms,
it appears to have a life of its own:
a dolmen round her childhood,
the standing stone
in the middle of the corn-
field, a totem, a sawn-off bone.

VII

The Chair

In the Queen's house
in Mount Charles

I took the chair,
you took the floor

in your burgundy
crushed-velvet flares

your platform clogs
and cheese-cloth shirt—

or was that me?
What did you wear?

Your corduroy maxi-skirt?
Were we burning joss sticks?

Playing *Horslips*?
It seems so long ago

I'm not quite sure.
I just remember

we were terribly thin
and you ate a satsuma

a thingammyjig,
a man—a mandarin.

I remember you remarked
on its dryness,

its lack of zest,
and you laid out its skin

in a circle, like the sun.
You rayed it

with burnt-out matches.
You patterned it

and played with it
in total silence

until night began to fall.
You raised your head:

'You think that you know me.
You really don't know me at all.'

THE AFTERMATH

Into the ringing silence
of this aftermath
surge the followers
of Michael Faraday,
Spinoza and St. Joseph.

Such urgent *putti*.
Their minds are troubled
by blockboard sheets, clout nails,
reels of cable, bags of putty,
holidays in the Bahamas.

Far away
the last burglar alarm on earth,
a hyperactive, bloody snail
on a trail of broken glass,
is going clean bananas.

THE ILLUMINATED MAN

Says, on the one hand, love,
but on the other, hate.
His left arm, fierce and brawny
as the femur of a saint,
is ice cold and encased
in a serpent
that coils on a dagger.

On his chest a faded heart,
pierced by another dagger,
surmounts the tawdry
of the legend MOTHER.
The semi-oriental
insomnia of his shoulder blades
is dragon-blue and sweating.

It's hard to tell
if the jaunty octopus
has the comely, couchant geisha girl
in its seven-fold and intimate embrace
against her will. Still it spares
from the toils of its intricate hold
one scrawny switch of tentacle

with which to seraph AMOR,
swagger VINCIT OMNIA.

COLONIST

I am the shoreline: you are the sea;
I am the lock: you are the key;

I am the slate: you are the felt;
I am *Anschauung*: you are *die Welt*;

I am the mirror: you are the face;
I am the colonist: you know your place;

I am the candle: you are the flame;
I can't describe it: you are the name;

I am the short of it: you are the long;
Were I a singer, you'd be the song;

I am pure bafflement: you are pure fight;
I am blind fury: you are a sight;

I am exhausted now: switch out the light.
I am exhausted now: switch out the light.

THE SECRET MISSION
for Bruce

He rises like a genie from an empty bottle,
one of a trail that dots and dashes the expanse
of the bedroom's sandstone Berber.
Something other than morning is in the air—
expensive perfume, a billow of silk
beneath his balloon-back chair.

He finds he simply can't remember
who she was last night,
that parachuted in, to blow his cover,
hell-bent on mischief, carrying a message
that would completely change his life.
Something about a room. Somewhere

about this room a lady is alive and in the pink.
A bubble zig-zags through
the dregs of an abandoned gin and tonic.
He massages an elbow
still raw from last night's coup.
There is a growing sense of panic.

SNOWCEM

There are times it seems
almost pointless
to write another word.

The obscure Russian sect had set aside
as marking the End of the World
the day I levered open
a four-year-old bin of Snowcem,
to Snowcem our back yard.

I decided to enjoy myself.
I took my hurry,
et in saecula saeculorum
I thought, as I slopped and slurried,
how perfectly
the Snowcem
slaked and hissed,
how perfectly I could get
it down on paper.

It might easily look like this:

CRATERS

I

I would have dismissed it as science fiction—
Earth: the Planet of the Twin Moons?
Really!—until tonight when
we called a temporary ceasefire.
She turned over the change
in the pocket of her jeans
and said, 'God bless the new moon ... '
Her words tailed off into silence.
A comet should, perhaps, have passed,
or a shooting star, as I looked higher
in the pitch black of my anger
beyond the double-glazing
at, yes—indeed there were—two moons,
both sickle-thin, both badly shaken.
She stormed straight out of the room
taking the door-knob by its fist,
the door almost lifted off its hinges,
leaving me pretending to be calm
and the twin moons quaking.

II

Sunday, bloody Sunday. Another deadline.
The children watching *Looney Toons* on *Sky*.
Enya singing backwards—*Shepherd Moons*.
'These papers! What happened yesterday,
what's to happen tomorrow, never
what's happening today. Will I read our stars?
Where are we? Gemini.' She unfolds her copy
of the *Sunday Life*, without waiting for the reply.
'All you've been hoping for, ever, is starting to come true ... '
She sneezes. ' ... God bless me!' 'God bless us all!'
I had riches all too great to count
and a high ancestral name. I catch
another blood-curdling headline
with the corner of my eye. 'You've heard the latest.
It's all come out, at last. I suppose you know already—
the man behind the mirror is a spy.' *But I also dreamt*
which pleased me most, that you loved me still the same,
that you loved me—'I suspected as much.'—
you loved me still the same. '*Did* you, now—did you *really*?'

III

'But which is the real moon?'
An *Inside Ulster* update on the television,
which watches us from the bay of the study window,
and we watch it—we seldom draw the curtains.
Beyond them, the twin moons, and beyond the moons
someone is speaking. 'Listen. Turn up the sound.' 'No!
Give me peace. I've more to do with my time—so
if you want me I'll be in the kitchen.'
Well, of course I want you! Some chance tonight
with politics, children, washing and ironing.
'What on earth comes closest to the infinite?'
'Ironing.' Did I really shout that out,
or was it simply going through my mind?
Did you shout back, 'Sometimes I love you, I think!'
Unfortunately, due to broadcasting restrictions
the voice was the voice of an actor in seamless lip sync
though someone was actually speaking—
the soundbite was double-think.
The words were dubbed, not mimed.

IV

Houdini said to get out of bed
was the hardest thing he could do.
Ash Wednesday: a day of fast and abstinence.
A meal and two collations. So what's new?
'Let's make a shopping list: *The Elixir of Life,*
The Philosopher's Stone, The Secret of the Universe,
The Universal Solvent?' 'Breakfast!'
A cup of pitch-black instant coffee,
two dazzling white aspirin, staring up at you:
the night sky and the twin moons of a planet
that certainly isn't Venus. 'Was he speaking to his wife?'
You stare back at me, your eyes like saucers. 'Who?'
'Houdini. Isn't it about time you changed those trousers?'
'Into what?' The hangdog look of Al Capone.
The Untouchables clicking on the bracelets.
'Don't let's let my trousers come between us.'
'Now that's more like it!' Eclipsed by lust,
the ash tray tips, the result of our collisions.
Your thumb cool on my forehead. *Remember thou art dust.*

V

'Earth to space station. Earth to space station.
Are you receiving me? Over. Come to bed!'
The bedroom is an exact replica of the study.
Stanza upon stanza. 'This could go on all night.'
I should be so lucky ! 'Leon! Come to bed!' '*Stanza*
from the Latin *sto*, starry, steady,
station—to stand.' 'Come to bed!' 'What for?
We'll only fight.' Her voice is a disembodied whisper
from the pitch-black of the stairs.
'Well then, at least let's fight.' 'Do you remember
that night in Sligo when he stared into the pitch-black
and mimed *Margaret, are you grieving?* across the theatre
staring directly at you—do you remember?'
'Yes, I remember.' 'Of course you do.
Didn't he sound precisely like a lover?'
'What does a lover sound like?' 'You remember.
Remember how the room lit up?' 'Who cares?' 'I do.'
'Just come to bed.' 'Why? Space station to earth, what for?
Are you receiving me? Are you receiving me? Over.'

[71]

VI

Ballynaclosha, Lugstown, town of the ear—
the stream that meanders past
the bottom of your Street is the actual Border,
but we know the state exactly that we're in.
This weekend, on a duty call to your mother,
we stroll across the river by the grey bridge in the hollow
built by our children's great-great—is that
too many greats?—grandfather. The Clogger Lavelle.
When you stop I wait. Where you lead I follow.
Down through the Rassan. Past the ancient milestone
to Dungooley, the Georgian farmhouse, kept like a palace
above the ruin of the mill: the twin moons of the giant millstones,
ears to the ground. Past rusted cogs and wheels within wheels,
up the servants' staircase we creak and rattle.
The rooms upstairs stuffed to the rafters with fodder,
the whole house ticking. Our mattress, our *palliasse*,
Rumpelstiltskin and the princess. Your father
asked one question. 'Do you love her?' 'I will give her my name
where dawn whitens Glassdrummond chapel.' Forever.

VII

Matins, Lauds. Sext, None. Vespers. Complan.
The blood-red lunar eclipse of the halogen hob,
when you slide the saucepan and turn the knob
to full. Another wasted night. Assured
though we may have been by Patrick Moore
that tonight the moon would turn to blood
we have no right to complain, or wish our lives away.
Had we listened to tonight's weatherman, Michael Fish,
a clear night, a full moon, we should have expected cloud.
But we dashed, unthinking, up the accustomed track
and bundled into the car. Bob Dylan sang *Ramona*.
We sat in the pitch-black lay-by for hours,
fielding metaphysical questions from the back
about the whos and the whys and the wherefores
of the myriad other gently-rocking cars.
'Did the weatherman *forecast* a hurricane?'
'Don't ever mention Fish to me again!'
'Saucepan!' You skim the rising, cream corona.
'That's it! Full stop! I'm through with cooking! Period.'

VIII

Last thing at night, arms round each other, we tip-toe in
to the cyber-space between their mountainous twin beds,
to tuck them in, to draw the blinds, turn down the radiator,
dim the light and gaze in luxurious wonder
at their shut-down, silken, phosphorescent heads.
The picture of ourselves. How peaceful now,
how far from *Menacer* and *Mortal Kombat*,
Sonic's desperate ring-quest: how far from cusps and nodes,
matrices, sets and mind-maps now they seem.
The window is furred with the image of their breathing.
Droplets network, in electronic streams and codes,
the virtual reality of perspex double glazing.
Goldfish. They dream in moons, whatever it is they dream.
Outside, steaming in, the halogen vapour streetlight
that lights the darkest corners of their childhood
limits the study of the stars. Caught in its jaundiced glow
we kiss each other. 'Goodnight.' 'Goodnight.'
We kiss, in turn, each haloed,
phosphorescent moon. And then we go.

IX

Visitors. And there we were, as usual, without a leg to stand on.
Caught. You with your arms sunk up to the oxters
in the children's bath. The dull thud of our broken doorbell.
Me swinging frantically on the fridge door. Fadge and soda,
wheaten, one rasher of bacon, a lamb chop from before Chernobyl
growing a beard in the corner, Enya singing backwards. A litre
carton of buttermilk I mistook for sweet. But sweeter
far, the makings of a fry. Apart from the eggs. 'Home
was never like this ... ' I was The Angel of Rome
and you were Venus de Milo, your arms now returned
from their parallel universe, and the twin moons
in which they had abruptly ended gone without trace.
The fridge door closed, the rasher of bacon in pitch darkness
with its *witenangemot* of left-overs, the lamb chop,
fadge and wheaten, *Dromona*, the carton of buttermilk.
A sunlit absinthe. We adopt a policy of dis-information, artifice
and second-best china. Earl Grey flavoured with bergamot:
'Chernobyl is Russian: Wormwood—Wormwood in Revelation.
Mugwort. Artemisia, the Greek for aftershave—from Artemis'.

X

And for our grand finale, in a fit of pique
you flounce in to the row that has erupted over dinner
and wheek the tablecloth from the table in a deft veronica,
sending into orbit, my cup of coffee, a couple of doo-wop CD's,
the perfume bottle, the box of Anadin, the house keys;
*Roget, Fowler, A Celtic Miscellany, The Penguin Dictionary
of Saints*, which lands on the unfinished family tree
Ben has for homework; the ornamental quill, the Belleek swan,
the loose leaf pad on which I am finishing this poem.
It flaps across the pitch black window, awkward, like a swan,
and down the back of the television, dislodging
the aerial, cutting off the weatherman in mid-
sentence as he witters on about a deep depression, tracking
south. Hurricane Alicia. What is most remarkable
about this unremarkable act of frustration
is how the vase of flowers, with the consummate ease
of an escapologist, the poise of a Buddha,
survives the ringing silence of the conflagration. You slump.
Your eyes are downcast. Your hands are limp between your knees.

XI

When, at last, I do get to sleep, predictably, I dream
of a rickety black-and-white space-ship landing on a moon.
Not our moon. A planet with its own two moons,
both mauve. From the porthole of my capsule
I descry a single crater. The moonscape is flashback purple,
monochrome. My retro-rockets splutter into life
and with a plume of pollen spore, I'm safely down.
I open the air-lock door to find that the purple cast has gone
and everything is blisteringly white: the aspirin moons
smile to each other at my embarrassment like nuns.
I take one giant step for mankind, land on my knees
and sink up to my haughs in lukewarm cottage cheese.
'Earth to space station. Are you receiving me?' A doom-
laden voice more distant than before, breaking with static.
My head crawls with hyperactive snails. I'm stumbling
away from a moonquake, when *bomb ba bomb bomb,*
ba bomb a bomb bomb, ba ba bomb ba ba bomb,
da dangy dang dang, de dingy dong ding, blue ...
strange, I think, to get *Radio Ulster* on the moon.